TRANSPORTATION THEN and NOW

Amanda Leitten

New York

Transportation means moving people
and things from place to place.

Transportation was different long ago.

How do you think it was different?

Then most people used horses
to move from place to place.

Now most people use cars
to move from place to place.

Then people used animals and wagons
to move things.

Now many people use big trucks
to move things.

Then people needed ships

to cross the sea.

The trip could take many weeks.

Now people cross the sea

in airplanes.

The trip only takes a few hours.

Even trains are very different today.

How do these trains look different?

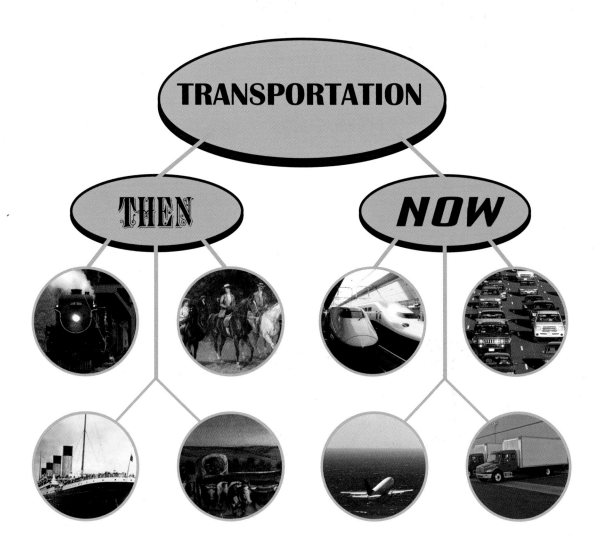

Words to Know

airplane

car

horse

ship

train

truck

wagon